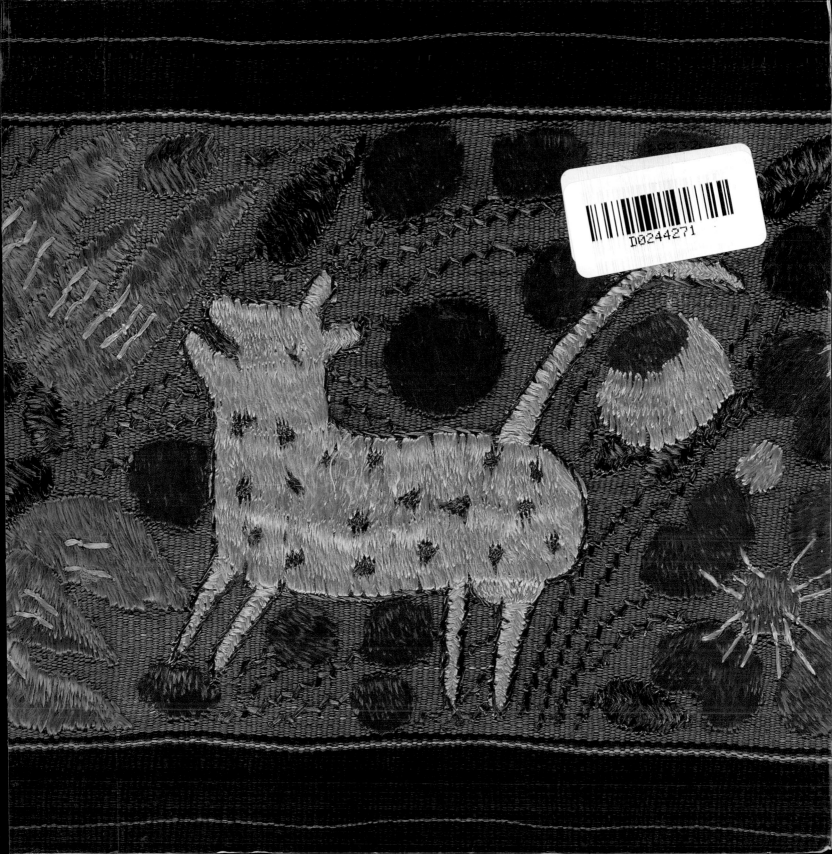

CHLOË SAYER

textiles from

mexico

THE BRITISH MUSEUM PRESS

First published in 2002 by The British Museum Press
A division of The British Museum Company Ltd
46 Bloomsbury Street, London WC1B 3QQ

A catalogue record for this book is available from the British Library

ISBN 0-7141-2562-8

Commissioning Editor: Suzannah Dick
Designer: Paul Welti
Editor: Caroline Brooke Johnson
Photographer: Mike Rowe
Cartographer: Olive Pearson
Origination in Hong Kong by AGP
Printing and binding in Hong Kong by C & C Offset

COVER: Detail of *huipil*; the Mixtec, San Miguel Metlatonoc, Guerrero. (See pp.62–3)
INSIDE COVER: Detail of Aguascalientes-style *sarape*. (See pp.60–1)
PAGE ONE: Detail of wrap-around skirt, the Nahua, Acatlán, Guerrero. (See pp.42–5)
PREVIOUS PAGE: Detail of *huipil*; the Tzotzil Maya, San Andrés Larrainzar, Chiapas.
THESE PAGES: Detail of ikat-dyed *rebozo*; Santa María del Río, San Luis Potosí. (See pp.46–7)

contents

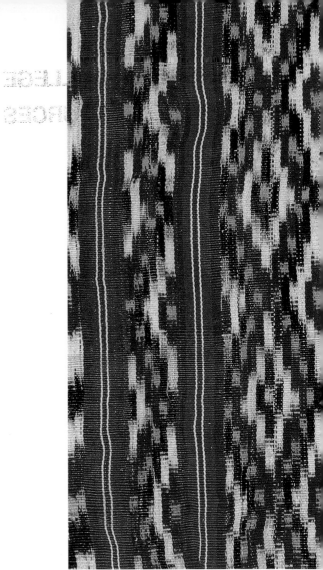

introduction 6

map 21

the design portfolio 22

glossary 82

selected reading 84

museum accession numbers 86

acknowledgements 86

picture credits 86

index 87

Opposite are details from a selection of textiles
TOP: Embroidered wrap-around skirt; the Nahua, Acatlán, Guerrero.
(See pp. 42–3)
LEFT: Brocaded white cotton bedspread; the Otomí, San Miguel
Ameyalco, State of Mexico. (See pp.26–7)
RIGHT: Densely embroidered *quechquemitl*; the Huichol, Jalisco. (See
pp.50–1)
BELOW: Cloth embroidered with satin stitch; the Otomí, Tenango de
Doria, Hidalgo. (See pp.34–5)

introduction

Few countries have such extreme variations
of climate and vegetation as Mexico.
Landscapes include arid deserts, fertile
valleys, tropical lowland forests, deep canyons
and high mountain peaks. Bordered by the
USA in the north, and by Guatemala and
Belize in the south-east, Mexico covers a vast
area of almost 2 million square km (760,000
square miles).

These contrasting environmental
conditions have influenced the evolution of
costume throughout Mexico's long history.
Stone carvings, terracotta figurines, murals

and painted manuscripts reflect this evolution, and show that ancient civilizations developed many different clothing styles. Today distinctive costumes are still worn in rural areas where indigenous cultures are strong. It is hard to establish reliable census figures in remote regions, but current estimates put Mexico's indigenous population – divided into fifty-six language groups – at around ten million.

The origins of the Maya go back more than 4,000 years. During their greatest period (AD 300–900), they excelled as architects, sculptors and astronomers. Maya civilization, based on a loose federation of city states, stretched across the Yucatán Peninsula and Chiapas in Mexico; it also took in Belize, Guatemala and parts of Honduras. Like their ancestors, the modern Maya speak many languages. In the highlands of central Chiapas, for example, there are over 133,000 speakers of Tzotzil.

To the west of the Maya zone, important cultures were forged after AD 300 by the Zapotec and the Mixtec. The present-day state of Oaxaca is home not just to their descendants, but to several other groups including the Trique, the Mazatec and the Chinantec. In Oaxaca, as in Chiapas, complex spinning, dyeing and weaving methods are still in use, passed down from generation to generation.

Huichol territory, high in the western Sierra Madre. The Huichol live in one of the most remote and rugged parts of Mexico. During the rainy season, the terrain becomes virtually impassable.

The most widely spoken indigenous languages in central Mexico are Otomí and Náhuatl. Náhuatl was the language of the Aztecs, who settled in the Valley of Mexico in the thirteenth century and built up a mighty empire. Today there are approximately 1,318,000 Nahua, as speakers of Náhuatl are now termed. They live in a number of states including Puebla, Veracruz, Hidalgo, Guerrero and San Luis Potosí. Natural surroundings provide basic building materials. Most families depend for their survival upon agriculture: the staple diet, as in ancient times, is made up of beans, squash, chilli peppers and maize.

Indigenous groups living in accessible areas have managed to retain many of their own traditions while adapting to Mexico's national culture. Other groups, in remote regions, continue to lead a surprisingly marginal existence. The Huichol survive high in the Sierra Madre, where the states of Jalisco and Nayarit meet. They have proved more resistant to outside pressure than most other groups, and the population now stands at around 50,000.

For the Huichol and for other indigenous peoples, textile skills centre chiefly on the creation of clothing. Contemporary textiles owe much of their richness to Mexico's ancient civilizations, but the European legacy should not be overlooked. After the Spanish Conquest of 1521, settlers introduced new materials, techniques and clothing styles. This fusion, over nearly five centuries, has given rise in Mexico to a wide range of garments and design motifs. In urban centres, boutiques and department stores provide city-dwellers with mass-produced factory clothing similar to that sold in London, Paris and New York. In outlying areas, however, indigenous people continue to take pride in home-produced clothing that reflects their cultural heritage while combining durability with beauty.

WOMEN'S COSTUME

In many regions, women's costume has changed very little since pre-Conquest times. Elaborately woven or embroidered clothing is worn every day, not just on ceremonial occasions. Wrap-around skirts are still widely used. Some are rectangular, but others are seamed to form a tube. Each morning, when the wearer puts on her skirt, she arranges the cloth in a series of folds or pleats. These are held in place by a waist-sash.

Also of pre-Conquest origin are the *huipil* and the *quechquemitl*. The *huipil* resembles a sleeveless, rectangular tunic made from one, two or three panels. Short garments may be tucked inside the skirt, but longer ones hang freely. The *quechquemitl* is best described as a closed shoulder-cape. Construction methods and styles of wearing vary from place to place. In ancient Mexico, the *huipil* and the *quechquemitl* coexisted in some regions and were occasionally worn together. Now each is found in separate areas.

Several European garments have found favour with indigenous women. These include

skirts on waistbands, aprons and blouses. Many blouses display large areas of embroidery. This is especially true in the Puebla highlands, where blouses are assembled from straight panels of bought cloth by the Nahua and the Otomí (see p.31 and p.38). So popular have blouses become that women in some *huipil*-wearing regions now give these ancient garments sleeve-like trimmings (see p.76).

Heads may be covered in strong sunshine with a specially woven cloth, a second *quechquemitl*, or, more rarely, a palm hat.

Tzotzil women in Oxchuc, Chiapas, wearing *huipiles* over indigo-dyed wrap-around skirts. In the foreground are two Tzeltal weavers from Tenejapa; both wear predominantly red *huipiles* patterned with brocading. All belong to a weaving co-operative.

The *rebozo* is a rectangular shawl, which offers protection and can double as a cloth used for carrying a load or a baby. Used in cities as well as rural areas, the *rebozo* evolved during the colonial period to become a national symbol of womanhood. Costly examples were, and still are, woven from ikat-dyed silk thread in Santa María del Río in the state of San Luis Potosí.

MEN'S COSTUME
AND OTHER TEXTILES

Male indigenous dress has undergone more changes than female dress. Before 1519 men wore loincloths, hipcloths, sashes, tunics, capes and imposing headdresses. After the Conquest, however, Spanish friars put pressure on their new charges to adopt shirts and trousers. In recent decades, economic hardship has forced many indigenous men to seek work far from home and to abandon their own garments in favour of jeans, T-shirts and baseball caps.

And yet, despite the pressure for change, some communities prefer traditional clothing styles. Shirts and trousers may be European in inspiration, but makers interpret them in various ways. Handsome examples are home-woven in the Chiapas highlands and in parts of Oaxaca; they are loose-fitting and made without zips, buttons or pockets. In most other areas, shirts and trousers are made from factory-produced cloth. Huichol men take enormous pride in their clothing with displays of colourful embroidery. Woven and embroidered shoulder-bags make up for the lack of pockets (see p.52). Trousers are held up with woven waist-sashes.

In cold weather, many men wear a woollen *sarape*, a rectangular blanket, often with an opening for the head. Like the *rebozo*, the *sarape* evolved while Mexico was under Spanish rule. After 1821, when Mexico became independent, foreign travellers likened the *sarape* to a 'national institution'.

Wealthy men wore splendid examples displaying complex geometric markings; some *sarapes* even incorporated silk, gold and silver metallic threads. Contemporary *sarapes* are more affordable but less ornate.

Although most indigenous textiles are made to be worn, great care goes into the

An Otomí boy in San Pablito, Puebla. Here he wears traditional clothing of factory-made cotton cloth, instead of the more usual T-shirt and jeans.

making of *servilletas* – all-purpose cloths, used to wrap or cover food. During religious festivals, they are displayed on altars in churches and homes.

Increasingly, traditional textile skills are used to produce non-traditional items that suit the needs and tastes both of Mexican city-dwellers and foreign tourists. Much-needed income is generated from the sale of tablecloths with matching napkins, wall-hangings and rugs, bedspreads and cushion covers. All too often purchasers value cheapness above quality. But examples of fine workmanship, like the bedspread shown on pp.26–9, are worthy of their place in the British Museum's collections.

RAW MATERIALS AND THEIR PREPARATION

White cotton is native to the New World; so too is the rarer, toffee-brown strain known as *coyuche*. Cotton is cultivated in hot and humid lowland regions and traded in highland areas. Preparation is long and arduous. Once the impurities have been removed by hand, the cotton is beaten with two wooden sticks until the fibres adhere together. As in pre-Conquest times, spinning is done with the aid of a spindle weighted with a clay whorl. Women sit on a low chair or kneel on a palm mat. With the left hand, they feed the fibres on to the tip of the spindle-shaft. With the right hand, they whirl the spindle in a dish or on level ground. Skilful spinners produce smooth and resistant

thread: without this, it would be impossible to weave durable, finely textured cloth.

After cotton, wool is the fibre most frequently used for indigenous clothing. Introduced into Mexico after the Conquest, it is especially popular in cold and mountainous regions. Women in Tzotzil communities in the Chiapas highlands are responsible for tending and sheering sheep. Washed wool is carded, as it once was in Europe, with a pair of boards inset with short wire bristles. It is then spun with a spindle. In weaving centres, however, woollen textiles are produced in large

Nahua weaver preparing *coyuche* (brown cotton) for spinning in Cuetzalan, Puebla. The cotton has been beaten until the fibres adhere together.

Nahua woman spinning white cotton with a spindle in San Andrés Tzicuilan, Puebla. She wears a gauze-woven *quechquemitl* of hand-spun white cotton over her embroidered blouse.

provides Mixtec women with silk. It is boiled in water with ashes, dried and then spun with a spindle. In most other regions, weavers and embroiderers rely on imported silk.

In recent decades, shortages and spiralling costs have forced many women to abandon natural fibres in favour of synthetic ones. Rayon serves as a cheap substitute for silk, while acrylic is fast replacing wool and can be re-spun for fine work. Francisca Rivera Pérez, seen on p.12 preparing *coyuche*, has this to say: 'Today we can buy yarns that are ready for the loom. Here in Cuetzalan we buy lustrous white thread for our weavings, and rainbow-coloured threads to embroider our blouses. But when I was growing up, we all learned how to spin. Our mothers would ask the Virgin Mary to help us. When I began to use a spindle I was thirteen, and I can remember even today how hard it was to learn.'

DYES AND DYEING

Chemical dyes have increasingly taken over from natural colourants since their invention in the nineteenth century. Fortunately natural dyes are still in use in some communities, however. This is true in the Chiapas highlands, where *huipiles* and waist-sashes often display a gamut of rich and subtle shades (see pp.78–81).

Traditional dyeing methods require great skill and patience, with operations taking several hours or even days. While some dyes stain fibres directly, others are fixed by mordants such as alum or urine. There is also

quantities and European spinning wheels are more commonly used.

Silk is greatly prized in indigenous Mexico. Although silk plantations were successfully established by Spanish settlers, they were later banned by royal decree when they threatened Spain's own silk industry. Fortunately, some insects and mulberry trees survived. Small-scale production in Oaxaca

a third dye category requiring oxidization. Weavers rarely measure their ingredients. They rely instead on intuition, preferring to work *al tanteo* (by guesswork).

Inorganic substances found in natural deposits play a vital role. Iron oxide, gypsum and ochres are mixed with other elements to provide stable dyes. In the Tzotzil community of San Juan Chamula, wool boiled with earth is stained a rich black. Localized plant dyes include flowers, fruits, roots, leaves and lichens. Reddish tones may be obtained with brazilwood. The plant species most widely used by dyers is indigo (*Indigofera anil*). Its deep blue hue is appreciated by skirt-weavers in the state of Chiapas. Here, cotton thread is repeatedly dipped in a watery solution of indigo and lye mixed with a plant called *sacatinta* (*Jacobinia spicigera*). After each soaking, the thread is hung up to dry so that the dye can oxidize. With every immersion, the colour deepens. When used without indigo, *sacatinta* produces a dark grey with purplish-blue overtones.

Two animal dyes, greatly valued before and after the Conquest, persist today. Cochineal (*Dactylopius coccus*) is a delicate insect which feeds on host cacti. When harvested and dried, these parasites provide colouring matter ideally suited to wool and silk. Depending on the type of mordant used, shades range from crimson to reddish-black. In Pinotepa de Don Luis and neighbouring Mixtec villages in Oaxaca, some wrap-around skirts still incorporate stripes of cochineal-dyed silk termed *hiladillo* (see pp.66–7). To weave these fine skirts Mixtec women also use indigo-dyed cotton, and lilac-coloured cotton dyed with the secretion of shellfish (*Purpura patula*). Along the shore of the Pacific, when the tide is low, colonies of molluscs are exposed to the gaze of dyers who pick them up and blow on them. The molluscs give off a colourless liquid which is rubbed directly on the thread. The air turns it yellow, then green and finally purple. The molluscs are returned to the rocks unharmed.

Until recently natural dyes such as indigo and cochineal were often used in conjunction with ikat. With this technique, threads are patterned before they are woven. Tightly bound at predetermined intervals, they are dipped in a dye bath. Covered areas are described as 'reserved'. If several colours are desired, the weaver will bind new sections and dip the threads in additional dye baths. Because no pre-Conquest examples of ikat have been found in Mexico, the technique is thought to have been introduced under Spanish rule. In the eighteenth century it was used to pattern *rebozos*, and this style of decoration remained popular after Independence in 1821. The Museum's collection includes two splendid late nineteenth-century examples: both display elegantly dappled markings (see pp.46–7). In Santa María del Río, where production continues of fine ikat-patterned *rebozos*, weavers work with silk or rayon. Near Toluca in central Mexico, they prefer cotton.

LOOMS AND WEAVING

Women weavers in indigenous villages make garments for themselves and their families using the native backstrap or stick loom. Although the apparatus is simple, with no rigid framework, it is extremely versatile and skilled weavers can create cloth of great beauty and complexity. Traditional garments are not tailored in the European manner; instead they are assembled directly from squares or rectangles from the loom. Texture and patterning are crucially important.

Because backstrap looms are easily rolled up and transported, most weavers work outside the house where there is space and light. Sometimes women gather together, chatting as they weave. Woven textiles are made by interlacing a series of threads, termed the 'weft', at right angles with a series of threads, termed the 'warp'. The warp is stretched between two end bars. When the loom is in use, one bar is tied to a tree or post; the other is attached by a strap to the weaver. Long webs of cloth can be woven on the backstrap loom, but the width is limited by the weaver's armspan. Although most women like to sit on a low chair or mat, they may kneel or stand when weaving heavy cloth.

As in pre-Conquest and colonial times, handsome effects are achieved with a variety of weaving techniques. When the warp and the weft are equal in thickness and number, the cloth is described as balanced. Warp- or weft-faced cloth occurs when the threads of one set are dominant.

Among Mexican backstrap weavers, the most widespread style of decoration is brocading. Often mistaken for embroidery, this superstructural technique was used to pattern many of the *huipiles* in this book. The Mixtec *huipil* on pp.62–3 features brocaded birds and plume-tailed horses created with supplementary weft threads of many colours. Tzotzil women in the Chiapas highlands are also adept at brocading cloth (see p.2 and pp.80–1). Although weavers carry the design in their heads, most like to keep old

Tzotzil women weaving with their backstrap looms in Oxchuc, Chiapas.

fragments of cloth that they can refer to for guidance.

Some of the garments included here incorporate areas of gauze-weaving (see pp.76–7). Selected warp threads have been crossed by hand and secured by the weft to create open-meshed cloth. In the highlands of Puebla, gauze-weavers create dazzling all-white *quechquemitl* with the delicacy of lace (see pp.12–13).

Sophisticated techniques like these require weavers to divide and subdivide warp threads in complex sequences. Older women

With backstrap looms, the width of the cloth is limited by the weaver's armspan.

in remote areas have often received little or no formal education, yet they reveal an intuitive grasp of mathematics as they pattern cloth with different motifs. The magnificently brocaded bedspread on pp.26–9 displays a multitude of animals, people, houses and flowers. It was woven in the Otomí village of San Miguel Ameyalco in the state of Mexico by Ana Cecilia Cruz Alberto. Asked to explain her rapid calculations, she replied: 'My fingers think for me. It is my fingers – not my head – that do the counting.' It takes many years to achieve this degree of skill. Girls in weaving families are expected to start learning the rudiments of their craft by the age of twelve.

The backstrap loom – in common with most other pre-Conquest methods of textile production – remains the preserve of women. The Spanish treadle loom, by contrast, is mostly worked by men. Faster than native looms, treadle looms can produce broader and longer webs of cloth. Small family-run workshops in many states provide local people with shawls, skirt lengths and *sarapes*, or blankets, of wool or acrylic yarn.

Tapestry weaving remains a popular method for patterning *sarapes*. Discontinuous weft threads cover the warp threads and form mosaic-like areas of colour: when the cloth is completed, these give a pattern or picture. Eighteenth- and nineteenth-century weavers in Saltillo, in the northern state of Coahuila, created dazzling effects. Characteristic designs included small triangles, rhomboids, hour-glasses and ovals grouped round a central lozenge or medallion (see p.54–9). Similarly patterned *sarapes* were produced in weaving centres in Querétaro, Zacatecas and San Miguel de Allende.

Few contemporary *sarapes* achieve the splendour and the complexity of the examples in this book, but great imagination and ingenuity are shown in Teotitlán del Valle, Oaxaca. Here Zapotec tapestry-weavers outline their designs on paper. Colourful *sarapes*, rugs and wall-hangings carry stylized flower, animal or bird motifs. Some weavers choose to interpret designs borrowed from pre-Conquest cultures or from European artists, such as Klee or Picasso, but Arnulfo Mendoza draws his inspiration from Saltillo-style *sarapes*. Sought after by collectors, the work of this celebrated Zapotec weaver is helping to revitalize tapestry-weaving skills for future generations.

EMBROIDERY AND OTHER DECORATIVE TECHNIQUES

Embroidery has a long history in Mexico. Archaeological cloth fragments prove that decorative stitching was sometimes used on pre-Conquest clothing. After the Conquest Spanish needlework skills were taught in mission centres, while further inspiration was provided by textiles imported from China and the Philippines. Today Mexican women embroider home-woven and bought cloth with a range of stitches and designs. Embroidery samplers serve as a teaching aid while girls are learning and as a reminder in later life.

A Zapotec gala costume from the Isthmus of Tehuantepec in Oaxaca. The velvet *huipil* and skirt are hand-embroidered in silk; the flounce is of hand-made lace. Although both garments date from the 1930s, the style remains unchanged.

Brightly coloured factory threads are an incentive to creativity. These include acrylic, mercerized cotton, silk and silk substitutes. Satin-stitched animals, birds, flowers and foliage embellish a range of garments. Satin stitching is also used to conceal cloth joins in many wrap-around skirts, *quechquemitl* and *huipiles* (see pp.76–7). In Tenango de Doria and San Pablito, Otomí women satin stitch small cloths and large wall-hangings for the tourist market (see pp.34–7). Running stitch, too, is put to decorative use. In highland Puebla, the neck and sleeve panels of blouses are elegantly worked by this method (see pp.30–1). Crossed stitches have had enormous impact in most regions of Mexico. In the Otomí village of San Pablito in Puebla, women combine cross and long-armed cross stitches to pattern *quechquemitl* and blouse panels (see pp.32–3). The Huichol garments included here also display a range of designs in cross stitch.

Sometimes embroiderers combine a variety of other stitches. This is true in the Nahua community of Acatlán, Guerrero, where gleaming synthetic silk thread covers the surface of wrap-around skirts with satin, stem and fishbone stitches (see p.42–5). During the week, many women protect this wealth of embroidery by wearing their skirts wrong-side out.

There are many other ways of embellishing garments. In the Chinantec village of San Felipe Usila, Oaxaca, brocaded *huipiles* are partially overpainted with purple dye (see pp.74–5). Garments in several places now incorporate factory-made ribbons: sometimes these are sewn down to conceal seams or to reinforce neck openings; often they hang down in colourful cascades (see pp.70–1). Fringes also adorn a number of garments. Many *rebozos* and waist-sashes have long warp ends that are elegantly finger-

knotted (see pp.48–9). In Santa María del Río, *rebozo*-weavers entrust this task to outworkers who memorize designs, which have evocative names like *arcos* and *rosas*. Drawn threadwork, which requires individual threads to be drawn out from the finished cloth, adds interest to some textiles (see pp.68–9). Love of ornamentation is further exemplified by the tassels and pom-poms that adorn the corners of shoulder-bags (see p.52). It is this mixture of ancient and modern, of tradition and innovation, that lends such vitality to Mexico's wide range of costumes.

PATTERN AND SYMBOLISM

Indigenous costume has never been static. Printed pattern sheets, offering peacocks and Western-style roses, are influencing design in several areas. Yet many of the motifs that characterize indigenous clothing are a genuine legacy inherited from earlier times. These include stepped frets, zigzag lines, hooks and other geometric forms. The magnificently brocaded *huipil* on pp.64–5 displays serrated X-motifs composed of triangles. It also displays double-headed birds. Found in many regions, this popular motif is at the centre of an academic debate. While some anthropologists regard double-headed birds as a pre-Conquest survival, others link them with the crowned Habsburg eagle of colonial times. As this difference of opinion shows, Mexican designs have a complicated history. Some undoubtedly derive from the ancient civilizations of Mexico, but many

Huichol pilgrims travel long distances to pay their respects to the goddess of the sea at San Blas, Nayarit. The woman in the foreground (left) wears a handsomely embroidered *quechquemitl* (see pp.50–1).

evolved after contact with Europe, the Near East, China and the Philippines.

Flowers and foliage adorn many garments and share this mixed heritage. Flowers with eight petals are especially popular. Vases or pots of flowers, often surrounded by birds, are a recurrent theme. In their most developed form such designs are described as 'trees of life'. Sacred trees were linked in pre-Conquest times with the four cardinal points (north, south, east and west), but the 'tree of life' motif is also found throughout the world.

Although some designs include human beings, the animal world is a richer source of decorative elements. Represented in this book are a host of creatures including rabbits, deer, dogs and serpents. In Santa María Zacatepec, shirts and trousers carry an embroidered menagerie of minuscule rabbits, squirrels, foxes and even scorpions (see pp.68–9). Birds, with one head or two, appear on textiles everywhere. Some designs are unequivocally European in their inspiration: horses, introduced into Mexico at the time of the Conquest, now pattern many garments.

With all these designs, representations range from the naturalistic to the highly stylized. Some designs are so stylized that they are indecipherable to outsiders. Research undertaken during the 1970s and 1980s in the Chiapas highlands provides an analysis of weaving symbols in Magdalenas and other modern Maya communities. According to Walter F. Morris and Martha Turok, designs perpetuate traditional agricultural and astronomical concepts. Diamonds are flat representations of the earth; their corners correspond to the four cardinal points, as well as to the four corners of the sky and the maize field (see p.2 and pp.80–1).

Designs in the Chiapas highlands reflect the fusion of indigenous and Christian beliefs that has taken place since the Conquest. For the Huichol, who have rejected Christianity, costume remains an expression of faith. Textile symbols link them with their many gods and serve as visual prayers (see pp.50–3). Zigzag lines that suggest lightning are associated with rain, while the deer is viewed as an incarnation of both maize and the hallucinatory cactus peyote. Today the Huichol may use modern materials to create many of their designs, but the beliefs that inspire them have changed very little since they were described by the anthropologist Carl Lumholtz over a century ago.

TRADITION AND CHANGE

Clothing is bound up with a range of social issues and is closely linked with the self-image of Mexico's indigenous population. For the Mexican tourist industry, 'quaint' customs and 'exotic' costumes are an obvious attraction. In real life, however, the Huichol and other groups face discrimination from local people who equate the wearing of traditional clothing with backwardness.

In order to avoid embarrassment and even mockery, villagers often abandon indigenous garments, or cover them with shop-bought ones, when visiting towns and cities. Television, which reaches most areas, has done little to reverse this trend. Advertisements and television programmes sometimes pay homage to past achievements by the Aztecs or the ancient Maya, but they rarely refer to the contemporary culture of Mexico's indigenous citizens. If and when they do, the context is not always flattering. A young Otomí girl in San Pablito explained this to me: 'We almost never see ourselves on television. If indigenous people appear at all in *telenovelas* [soap operas] they seem always to be servants or cleaners.' Unsurprisingly, the speaker has cut her long hair and exchanged her embroidered blouse and wrap-around skirt for a T-shirt and jeans.

It would be tragic if indigenous dress, together with textile skills that have endured for centuries, should disappear altogether from Mexico. One sign of hope may lie with the Zapatistas: followers of the Zapatista movement in Chiapas see traditional clothing as an integral part of their identity and a reason not for shame but pride. Even tourism, so often blamed for a decline in standards, can have a positive effect: the embroidered wall-hangings on pp.34–7 were made to sell, yet they successfully combine commerce with joyful exuberance and freedom of expression.

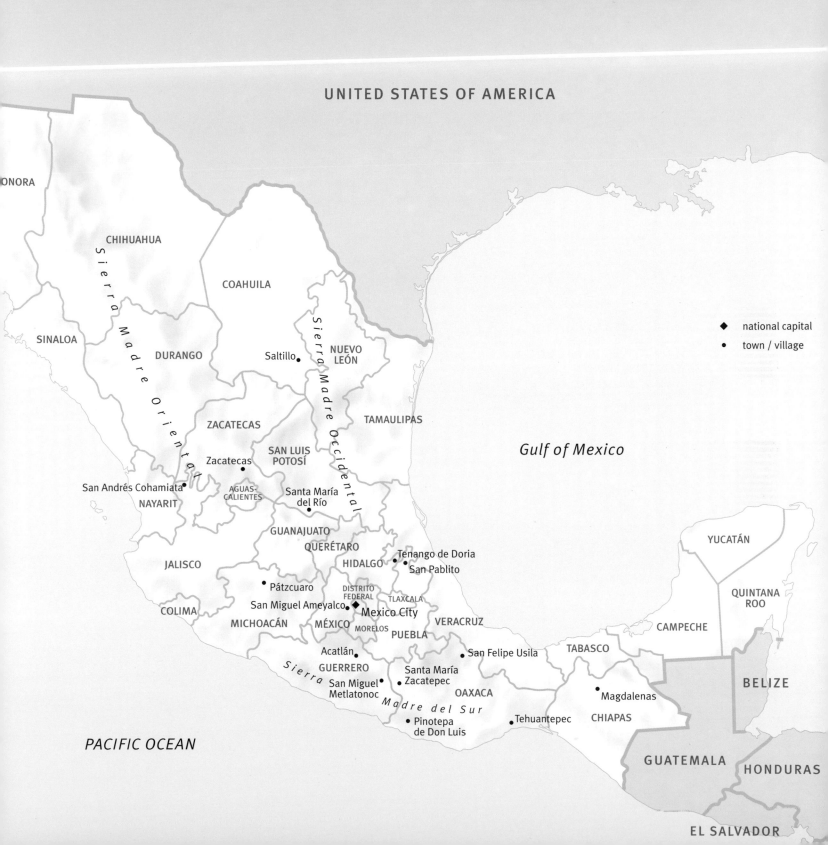

UNITED STATES OF AMERICA

SONORA

CHIHUAHUA

SINALOA

COAHUILA

Sierra Madre Oriental

DURANGO

Saltillo •

NUEVO LEÓN

ZACATECAS

Sierra Madre Occidental

TAMAULIPAS

Gulf of Mexico

Zacatecas •

SAN LUIS POTOSÍ

◆ national capital
• town / village

San Andrés Cohamiata •

AGUAS-CALIENTES

Santa María del Río •

NAYARIT

GUANAJUATO

QUERÉTARO

YUCATÁN

JALISCO

Pátzcuaro •

HIDALGO

Tenango de Doria •
• San Pablito

QUINTANA ROO

COLIMA

DISTRITO FEDERAL

San Miguel Ameyalco •
◆ Mexico City

TLAXCALA

VERACRUZ

CAMPECHE

MICHOACÁN

MÉXICO

MORELOS

PUEBLA

TABASCO

BELIZE

Acatlán •

GUERRERO

Sierra

San Miguel Metlatonoc •

Santa María Zacatepec •

San Felipe Usila •

Magdalenas •

OAXACA

CHIAPAS

Madre del Sur

Tehuantepec •

PACIFIC OCEAN

• Pinotepa de Don Luis

GUATEMALA

HONDURAS

EL SALVADOR

EMBROIDERED CLOTH
Woven over a century ago,
this all-wool single-panel textile was probably
used as a tablecloth.

Although the collector,
Robert Everts, kept no record of its
provenance, this textile shares many
stylistic features with contemporary work
by the Mazahua who live near Villa de Allende
in the State of Mexico. Designs, organized with
perfect symmetry, are embroidered in cross,
long-armed cross and herringbone stitches.
The complex border incorporates foliage and
bird motifs; the zigzag line that separates
them is inverted at each apex.
248 × 138 cm (98 × 54$\frac{1}{2}$ in)

FIGURATIVE MOTIFS RENDERED IN SIMPLE
BLACK AND BLUE ARE ARRANGED IN A LOOSE
BUT SYMMETRICAL PATTERN, CONTRASTING
WITH THE DENSE FLORAL BORDER. MOTIFS
INCLUDE AN ANTLERED DEER WITH A FLOWER
IN ITS MOUTH, AND A CHEQUERBOARD
HORSE. 'TREE OF LIFE' DESIGNS ABOUND.
THIS TERM DESCRIBES THE STYLIZED TREES
AND POTS OF FLOWERS, OFTEN SUR-
ROUNDED BY EXOTIC BIRDS, WHICH RECUR
IN MEXICAN TEXTILES.

A POWERFUL ZIGZAG LINE, INVERTED AT EACH APEX, SEPARATES STYLIZED FLOWER MOTIFS; A NARROW PATTERNED BORDER RUNS, LIKE

A MIRROR IMAGE, ALONG THE OUTER EDGES. THE STRONG CONTRAST OF BLUE AND WHITE REINFORCES THE BOLDNESS OF THE OVERALL DESIGN.

WOMAN'S SASH
Waist-sash with warp-brocaded designs
woven on a backstrap loom from white cotton and blue acrylic yarn.

The Mazahua excel at weaving sashes. These are ring-woven to form a
continuous band; designs are created with supplementary warp threads.
The warp ends, severed and twisted to prevent unravelling, are tucked
out of sight when the sash is worn. The top side is shown on the right;
designs may be seen in the negative on the reverse (left).
300 × 10 cm (118 × 4 in)

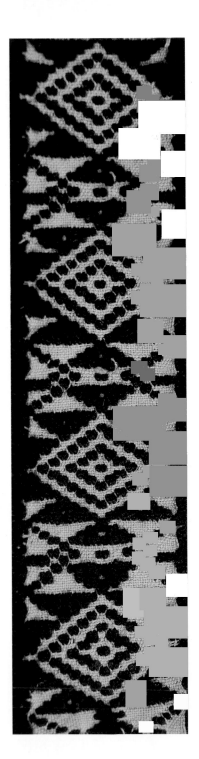

THIS BELT'S BLACK AND WHITE DESIGNS APPEAR TO MUTATE INTO
EACH OTHER SO SMOOTHLY THAT THE EYE BARELY REGISTERS THE
TRANSITION. AS ON THE SASH OPPOSITE, A ZIGZAG LINE AND THE
EIGHT-PETAL FLOWER MOTIF ARE INCORPORATED.

WOMAN'S SASH
Waist-sash with geometric designs woven on a
backstrap loom from white cotton with black and wine-coloured wool.

Purépecha women near Lake Pátzcuaro require strong waist-sashes to
hold up their voluminous pleated skirts of heavy wool. Complex designs
are created with selected warp threads. Warp ends are plaited by hand
and bound; when the sash is worn, they are tucked out of sight.
356 × 7 cm (140 × 3 in)

THIS COMPLEX DESIGN INCORPORATES HORIZONTAL BANDS OF PICTORIAL MOTIFS WITHIN FORMAL BORDERS. THE SUBJECT MATTER IS REPEATED IN EVER-CHANGING COLOURS WITH SCANT REGARD FOR SCALE. DEER ARE THE SAME SIZE AS CHURCHES; HORSE RIDERS ARE HARDLY LARGER THAN ROSES. DESPITE THIS THE

BEDSPREAD
Four-panel bedspread of white cotton brocaded with brightly coloured acrylic yarns.

Woven in four vertical panels on a backstrap loom by Ana Cecilia Cruz Alberto in 1977, this unusually large textile is weft-brocaded with a virtuoso display of birds, animals, flowers, churches and human figures. The exuberant design was inspired by the brocaded panels of cloth, termed *ayates*, that are worn by male dancers during local festivals. The weaver works without a pattern.
282 × 265 cm (111 × 104¹/₂ in) excluding fringes

BEDSPREAD HAS A STRONG VISUAL UNITY. THE WEAVING PROCESS, WHEREBY THE WEFT INTERSECTS AT RIGHT ANGLES WITH THE WARP, DETERMINES THE ANGULAR APPEARANCE OF THESE BRO-CADED DESIGNS, ACHIEVED BY THE CAREFUL COUNTING OF THREADS. MOTIFS INTER-LOCK INGENIOUSLY ON A WHITE BACKGROUND.

BLOUSE
Blouse of factory cotton cloth
embroidered in pattern running stitch with cotton thread.

In the Puebla highlands, blouses are unfitted. Fashioned from
straight cloth panels, they have square necklines and box-like sleeves.
Each embroidered panel is worked separately. When the blouse is
assembled, the cloth below the yoke is gathered into tiny pleats.
Cloth joins are emphasized with decorative stitching. This fine
example, which dates from the early 1980s, features
geometric designs and stylized plant motifs. This style
of embroidery closely resembles brocading.
59 × 53 cm (23 × 21 in)

(OPPOSITE) EMBROIDERED SLEEVE PANELS DISPLAY THREE
DIFFERENTLY PATTERNED BANDS. A ZIGZAG LINE, INVERTED AT EACH
APEX, SEPARATES THE DESIGN UNITS. THESE ARE ALTERNATELY
REVERSED AS THEY TRAVEL ALONG EACH BAND. THE SYMMETRY IS
ENHANCED BY THE USE OF A SINGLE COLOUR THAT STANDS OUT
AGAINST THE WHITE BASE CLOTH.

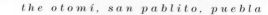

QUECHQUEMITL
Cotton and wool *quechquemitl*, woven in
two panels on the backstrap loom. In San Pablito,
quechquemitl are worn with the points to the sides.

The art of curved weaving, now rare,
has been used to make this *quechquemitl*: by converting
a group of warp threads to weft, the weaver has shaped the
pink band so that it curves at one end. The designs are
worked in cross stitch and long-armed cross
stitch on a plain-woven ground.
39 × 85 cm (15$^{1}/_{2}$ × 33$^{1}/_{2}$ in)

THIS DESIGN IN A POWERFUL COMBINATION OF COLOURS
USES PATTERN ELEMENTS ARRANGED SYMMETRICALLY.
THE POPULAR EIGHT-POINT STAR OR FLOWER MOTIF IS
RENDERED HERE IN A VARIETY OF WAYS. INTERLOCKING
SECTIONS CONTAIN STEPPED-FRET MOTIFS AND OTHER
GEOMETRIC FORMS.

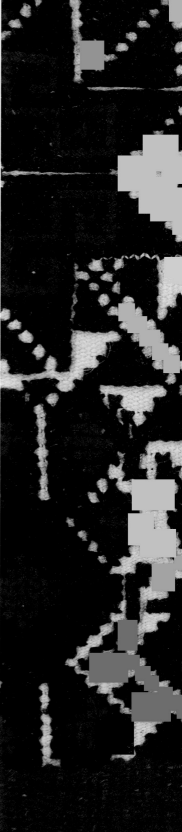

EMBROIDERED CLOTH
Factory cloth embroidered in satin
stitch with mercerized cotton thread.

For several decades, Otomí women
in Tenango de Doria and San Pablito
have earned much-needed revenue by
embroidering imaginative and often
fantastical landscapes. This example, produced *c.* 1977,
displays a wealth of plant designs and hybrid creatures.
152 × 107 cm (60 × 42 in)

THE APPARENT SIMPLICITY AND 'NAÏVE' CHARM OF
THIS WORK ARE DECEPTIVE. IT TAKES ENORMOUS SKILL
TO POSITION RANDOM FIGURES IN SPACE, YET ACHIEVE
AN OVERALL SENSE OF BALANCE AND HARMONY.

EMBROIDERED CLOTH
Factory cloth embroidered in satin stitch with mercerized cotton thread.

Before starting work, most women draw the outline of their designs freehand on to the cloth with a ballpoint pen. Although some stitches are very long, this is an economical form of satin stitch because threads travel back across the surface – not the underside – of the cloth. Like the previous example, this vibrant and highly decorative landscape was embroidered *c*. 1977.
180 × 72½ cm (71 × 28½ in)

BOLDLY EXECUTED RED AND BLACK MOTIFS ARE ASYMMETRICALLY POSITIONED TO FORM A HUMOROUS YET HARMONIOUS COMPOSITION. THIS DESIGN IS A UNIQUE CREATION ALTHOUGH THE TYPES OF ELEMENTS USED HERE ARE FOUND ON MANY SUCH CLOTHS.

BLOUSE
Nahua blouse of factory cotton cloth embroidered
with blue artificial silk yarn and red cotton thread.

Fashioned from straight cloth panels, this blouse
combines two distinct styles of decoration. Blue areas
have been hand-embroidered in pattern running stitch
to show birds, animals and flowers. Red areas have
been patterned on a sewing machine to display
spirals, leaves and other organic forms. A
frill has been added below the yoke.
70 × 68 cm (27¹/₂ × 27 in)

THE EMBROIDERY IS SO DENSE THAT THE FEW
WHITE AREAS THAT REMAIN CREATE THE DESIGN.

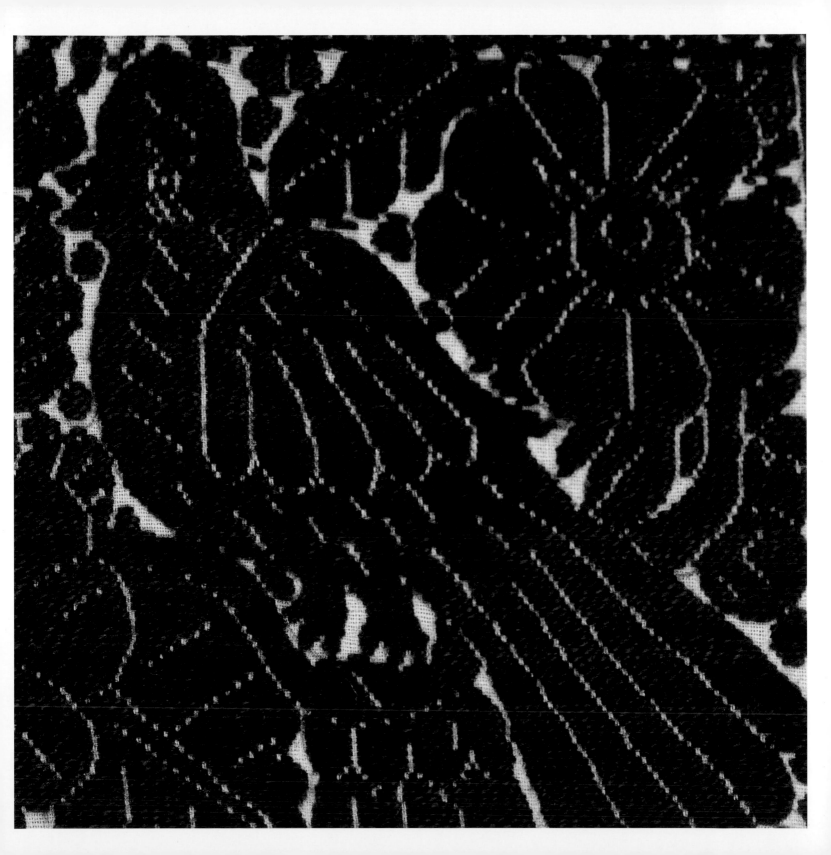

QUECHQUEMITL
Quechquemitl assembled from two panels of
home-woven cloth with weft-brocaded and
embroidered designs.

Near San Pedro Coyutla, older women
still wear the *quechquemitl* without a blouse
underneath. Raised weft-brocaded bands
of decoration run along the shoulder line. These
incorporate diamond and hook motifs, which are
older by far than the figurative designs. Worked in
cross stitch, these include a basket of flowers and
three lions with flowers on their heads.
36 × 97 cm (14 × 38 in)

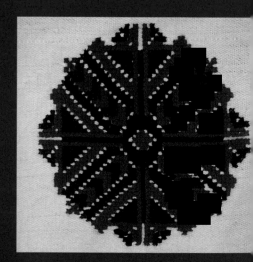

THE LIMITED USE OF COLOUR TO A BASIC RED AND
BLACK IS LIFTED BY THE OCCASIONAL INSERTION OF
BRIGHT PINK. DECORATIVE STITCHING MAKES A
DESIGN FEATURE OF THE CLOTH JOINS.

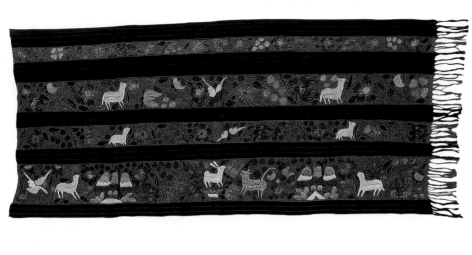

THIS SKIRT ABOUNDS WITH CHARMING ANIMALS, BIRDS AND FLOWERS. IT ALSO
INCLUDES MEXICO'S NATIONAL EMBLEM, SHOWN TWICE ALONG THE LOWER BAND, IN
THE FORM OF AN EAGLE, PERCHED ON A PRICKLY PEAR, WITH A SERPENT IN ITS BEAK.

WRAP-AROUND SKIRT
Embroidered wrap-around skirt, woven
in two panels on a backstrap loom with indigo-dyed cotton.

The skirt has pale blue and dark blue warp bands. Pale blue bands carry a wealth
of designs bordered by the dark blue bands. The embroiderer has used synthetic silk thread
and a combination of satin and couching techniques. For extra show, women sometimes add
sequins, which glint in the sunshine. On weekdays, many women protect this
delicate embroidery by wearing their skirts wrong-side out.
218 × 99 cm (86 × 39 in) excluding fringes

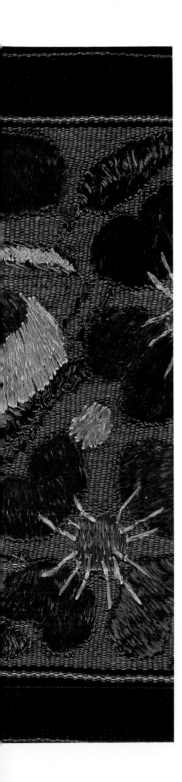

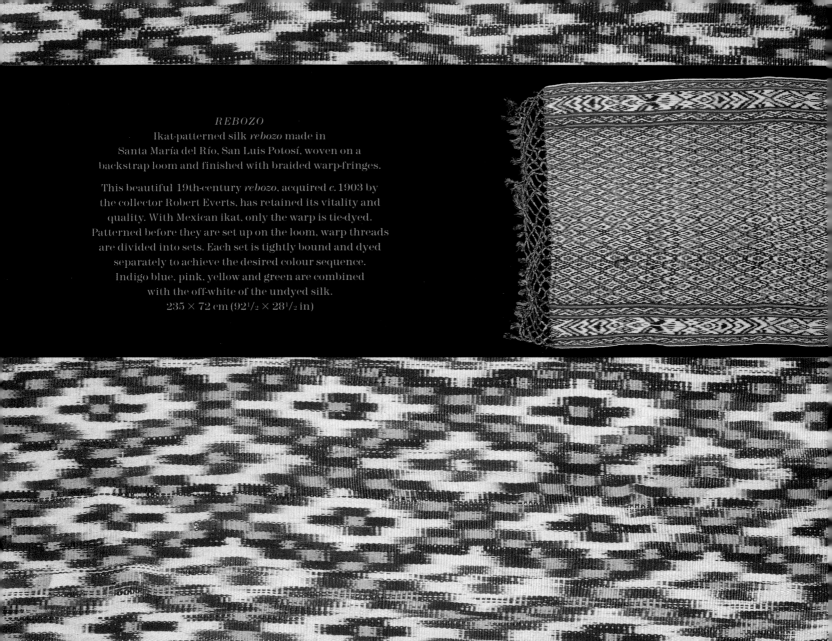

REBOZO

Ikat-patterned silk *rebozo* made in
Santa María del Río, San Luis Potosí, woven on a
backstrap loom and finished with braided warp-fringes.

This beautiful 19th-century *rebozo*, acquired *c.* 1903 by
the collector Robert Everts, has retained its vitality and
quality. With Mexican ikat, only the warp is tie-dyed.
Patterned before they are set up on the loom, warp threads
are divided into sets. Each set is tightly bound and dyed
separately to achieve the desired colour sequence.
Indigo blue, pink, yellow and green are combined
with the off-white of the undyed silk.
235 × 72 cm (92$\frac{1}{2}$ × 28$\frac{1}{2}$ in)

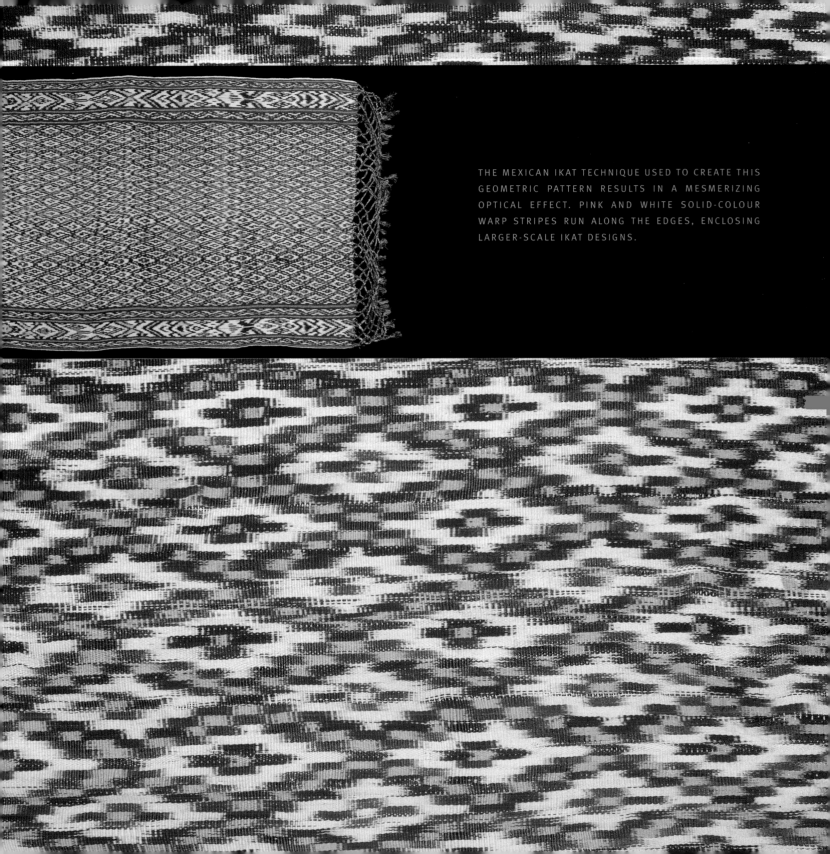

THE MEXICAN IKAT TECHNIQUE USED TO CREATE THIS GEOMETRIC PATTERN RESULTS IN A MESMERIZING OPTICAL EFFECT. PINK AND WHITE SOLID-COLOUR WARP STRIPES RUN ALONG THE EDGES, ENCLOSING LARGER-SCALE IKAT DESIGNS.

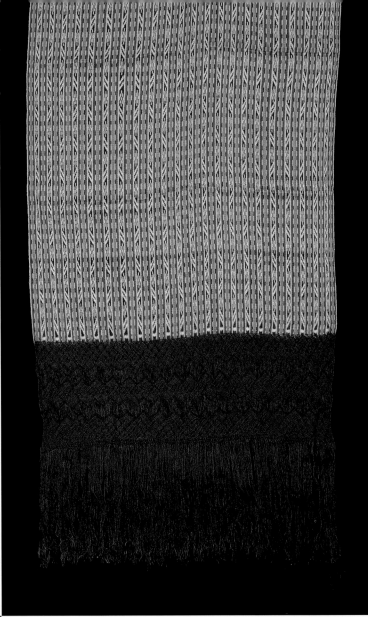

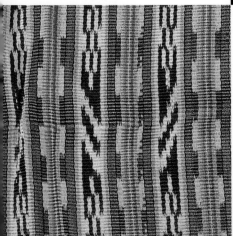

AS IN THE PREVIOUS *REBOZO*
THE IKAT TECHNIQUE PRODUCES
A SIMILAR 'BLURRED' EFFECT.
THE COLOURFUL MAIN AREA

CONTRASTS HARMONIOUSLY
WITH THE SINGLE COLOURED
BROWN HAND-KNOTTED FRINGE,
WITH ITS SUBTLE PATTERNING.

REBOZO

Ikat-patterned *rebozo* of artificial silk made
in Santa María del Río, San Luis Potosí. Woven on a
backstrap loom, it displays long finger-knotted warp fringes.

This *rebozo*, made in the 1980s, is separated by a century
from the previous example. The colours are less subtle, but the
artistry of contemporary ikat-dyers remains impressive.
Warp fringes are longer and considerably more
decorative than they were formerly.
268 × 63 cm (105$^{1}/_{2}$ × 25 in)

QUECHQUEMITL
Embroidered *quechquemitl*, made
by the Huichol people, Jalisco. It is assembled
from two square panels of open-meshed factory cloth.

Huichol clothing is more decorated than it was a century ago,
due mainly to the use of commercial threads. This garment is
dominated by a wide band of embroidery, worked in cross,
long-armed cross and herringbone stitches. There is a powerful
tension between the colours. Along the outer edge, for
example, the red and the green seem to vibrate together.
66 × 62 cm (26 × 24^1/$_2$ in)

MANY HUICHOL DESIGNS ARE STYLIZED TO THE POINT OF ABSTRACTION. TO THE RIGHT IS A ROW OF FOUR-HEADED EAGLES. TWO HEADS EXTEND FROM THE TOP OF EACH RECTANGULAR BODY; THE OTHER TWO HEADS, LIKE A MIRROR IMAGE OF THE FIRST TWO, STRETCH DOWNWARDS.

IN CONTRAST WITH THE FLAT EDGES OF THE INNER BORDER THE OUTER BORDER HAS BEEN ENLIVENED BY A ROW OF SILHOUETTED ANIMALS, INCLUD-ING A SINGLE RABBIT. THE BIRDS ARE THOUGHT TO HAVE MAGICAL POWERS – THEY CAN SEE AND HEAR EVERYTHING AS THEY FLY ABOVE THE EARTH.

MAN'S SHOULDER-BAG
Bag of white cotton cloth
densely embroidered in cross stitch and
long-armed cross stitch. The shoulder-strap
was woven on a backstrap loom.

Such bags make up for the lack of pockets
in Huichol clothing. Interlocking geometric
designs and juxtapositions of brilliant colour
are inspired by the peyote cactus. A potent
hallucinogen, peyote acts upon the brain's
visual cortex: visions, remembered long
afterwards, are imbued with kaleidoscopic
colours and geometric imagery.
22 × 24 cm (8$^{1}/_{2}$ × 9$^{1}/_{2}$ in) excluding
handle and pom-poms

WHILE THE WHITE CLOTH IS ALMOST TOTALLY
HIDDEN BY EMBROIDERY, YELLOW AREAS GIVE
THE ILLUSION OF BEING THE GROUND AGAINST
WHICH ALL THE OTHER FIGURES ARE SEEN.

THE EAGLE BELONGS TO GRANDFATHER FIRE AND GUARDS THE YOUNG MAIZE. IT MAY BE SHOWN IN PROFILE WITH A SINGLE HEAD, OR FROM THE FRONT WITH TWO HEADS TO REPRESENT BOTH PROFILES. ABOVE, THE BODY OF THE BIRD ENCLOSES AN EIGHT-PETALLED *TOTÓ* FLOWER. THIS IS A NATURALISTIC VERSION OF THE DESIGN OPPOSITE. THE WHITE OF THE CLOTH, ENCLOSED BY LINES OF STITCHING, IS A VITAL PART OF THE DESIGN.

THE *TOTÓ* FLOWER IS SEEN HERE IN AN EXTREMELY STYLIZED FORM WITH EIGHT ANGULAR PETALS. BECAUSE THE *TOTÓ* GROWS DURING THE WET, MAIZE-PRODUCING SEASON, IT IS BOTH A PETITION FOR AND A SYMBOL OF MAIZE. PEYOTE CACTUS IS AN INCARNATION OF MAIZE, SO THIS POPULAR DESIGN IS ALSO IDENTIFIED WITH PEYOTE. A ROW OF FLOWERS, IN ALTERNATING RED AND BLUE THREAD, DECORATES THE LOWER AREAS OF THE TROUSERS.

SHIRT AND TROUSERS
Open-sided shirt and trousers made
with factory-made cloth and cotton embroidery threads.

Huichol men are renowned for the splendour of their clothing.
Shirts and trousers are assembled from straight panels of factory
manta, or calico. *Manta* is hard-wearing, but it is more difficult to
embroider than open-meshed cloth (see pp.50–1). Figurative elements
such as birds dominate both garments: interlocking S-shaped motifs
and other geometric designs form decorative bands and borders. Both
garments are decorated in cross stitch and long-armed cross stitch.
Shirt: 104 × 150 cm (41 × 59 in) across arms
Trousers: 94 × 55 cm (37 × 21¹/₂ in)

SARAPE

Saltillo-style *sarape*, woven in two
panels on a treadle loom with a wool weft,
possibly from Saltillo, Coahuila.

Tapestry weaving gives this *sarape* its distinctive
patterning. During the colonial period, Saltillo
became the most famous production centre.
Later the term 'Saltillo' was applied to similarly
patterned *sarapes* from other towns. This fine
19th-century example displays small lozenges
and other interlocking geometric elements
grouped round a diamond centre. When the
sarape is worn, the patterning is vertical.
224 × 116 cm (88 × 45¹/₂ in)

BY MANIPULATING RICHLY COLOURED THREADS,
TAPESTRY-WEAVERS ACHIEVED DAZZLING MOSAIC
EFFECTS DESCRIBED BY NÁHUATL-SPEAKERS AS
ACOCEMALOTIC-TILMATLI (RAINBOW-MANTLES).

SARAPE

Saltillo-style *sarape*, tapestry-woven in two panels on
a treadle loom. Acquired *c.* 1903, it dates from the 19th century.

According to some estimates, the weaving of a fine *sarape* could
have required up to 500 hours. Complex patterning was probably achieved
with the help of painted pattern boards. The woollen weft
yarns were left natural, or dyed with cochineal and vegetable
colourants such as indigo and brazilwood.
227 × 120 cm (89$^1/_2$ × 47 in)

PRACTICAL YET HIGHLY DECORATIVE, THIS FINE *SARAPE* IS
PATTERNED IN CLASSIC SALTILLO STYLE WITH INTERLOCKING
GEOMETRIC ELEMENTS; THESE ARE GROUPED AROUND A
SERRATED CONCENTRIC DIAMOND AT THE CENTRE.

SARAPE

This 19th-century Saltillo-style *sarape* is tapestry-woven in two
panels on a treadle loom with a wool weft and a finger-knotted warp fringe.

Popular in country areas, the *sarape* was described by one
19th-century observer as 'convenient and graceful, especially on horseback'.
The wearer could use it like a cape; in cold and wet weather, he could put
his head through the slit and become a 'moving tent'.
230 × 133 cm (90½ × 52½ in) excluding fringes

THE ABSTRACT PATTERNING OF MANY *SARAPES* SEEMS TO OSCILLATE AND TO
PLAY GAMES WITH THE RETINA. HERE, POSITIVE AND NEGATIVE ELEMENTS ARE
SO PERFECTLY BALANCED THAT THE EYE VEERS CONSTANTLY BETWEEN THE
FIGURES IN BROWN AND BLUE AND THE UNDYED GROUND.

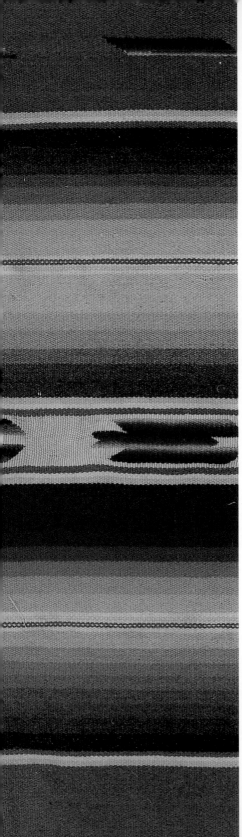

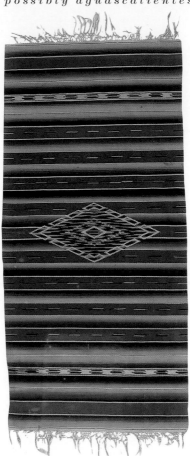

SARAPE

Aguascalientes-style, tapestry-patterned
sarape. Woven as a single panel on a treadle loom with
shaded wool, it has a short finger-knotted warp fringe.

Although there is no date of manufacture, this aniline-
dyed *sarape* was probably made during the late 19th
century. Yarn was delicately shaded for the weft stripes
by a process known as *ombré* dyeing. Each skein was
dipped in a colour, dried off, then partially
re-dipped in a stronger solution. Successive
dippings produced the desired shading.
196 × 91 cm (77 × 36 in) excluding fringes

IN THIS EXAMPLE THE LOZENGE PLAYS A LESS IMPORTANT
ROLE IN THE OVERALL DESIGN, ALLOWING THE BACK-
GROUND TO HAVE A POWERFUL IMPACT.

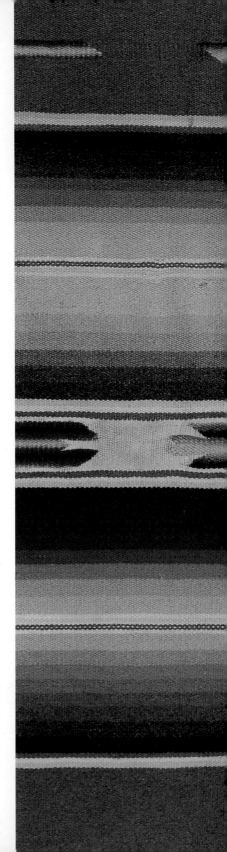

HUIPIL (FRONT AND BACK)
Three-panel gala *huipil*, woven on a backstrap loom from
hand-spun cotton. Designs are brocaded with commercial cotton thread.

Brightly coloured brocaded motifs include geometric elements, birds
with outstretched wings, double-headed eagles, and rearing horses with
plumed tails (see detail below). Interlocking diamond motifs pattern the
shoulder line and part of the central panel. Much-worn, this *huipil* has
been reinforced at the neck with a narrow section of embroidered cloth.
Panels are joined with decorative insertion stitching.
79 × 98 cm (31 × 38½ in)

THIS SPLENDID AND HIGHLY DECORATED GARMENT IS UNUSUAL IN THAT IT HAS BEEN WOVEN WITH
ALMOST NO REGARD FOR SYMMETRY. EACH PANEL HAS BEEN CONCEIVED INDIVIDUALLY.

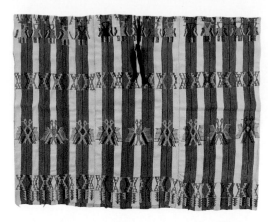

HUIPIL
Three-panel ceremonial *huipil* with brocaded motifs.
It was woven on a backstrap loom during the early 1970s.

The weaver has used hand-spun white cotton, lilac cotton dyed with the
secretion of shellfish, and *hiladillo* (cochineal-dyed silk). The neck
opening is edged in satin ribbon. Such garments are worn for the
marriage ceremony or by the wives of dignitaries.
104 × 133 cm (41 × 52$\frac{1}{2}$ in)

THE STRENGTH OF THIS DESIGN LIES IN ITS USE OF
SYMMETRY WITH STYLIZED BROCADED MOTIFS
RUNNING HORIZONTALLY ACROSS THE WARP
BANDS. MOTIFS INCLUDE TWO VERSIONS OF
DOUBLE-HEADED BIRDS (BELOW AND RIGHT).

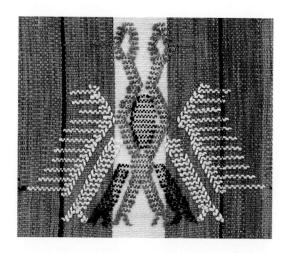

WRAP-AROUND SKIRT

Three-panel *posahuanco*, or wrap-around
skirt, woven on a backstrap loom with warp stripes.

Woven in the early 1970s, this splendid textile incorporates
hiladillo (cochineal-dyed silk), dark blue cotton dyed with
indigo, and lilac cotton dyed with the secretion of shellfish.
Weavers in Pinotepa de Don Luis provide several local
communities with skirts; subtle variations in
the width and distribution of stripes
distinguish each community.
182 × 119 cm (71½ × 47 in)

WRAP-AROUND SKIRTS ARE OFTEN PATTERNED WITH WARP
STRIPES. SKIRTS FROM THE PINOTEPA REGION, WITH THEIR
RICH COLOURING, ARE AMONG THE FINEST IN MEXICO. THE
VARIATION IN COLOUR RESULTING FROM THE DIFFERING
ABSORPTION OF DYE BY THE FIBRES GIVES THE TEXTILE
ADDED DEPTH.

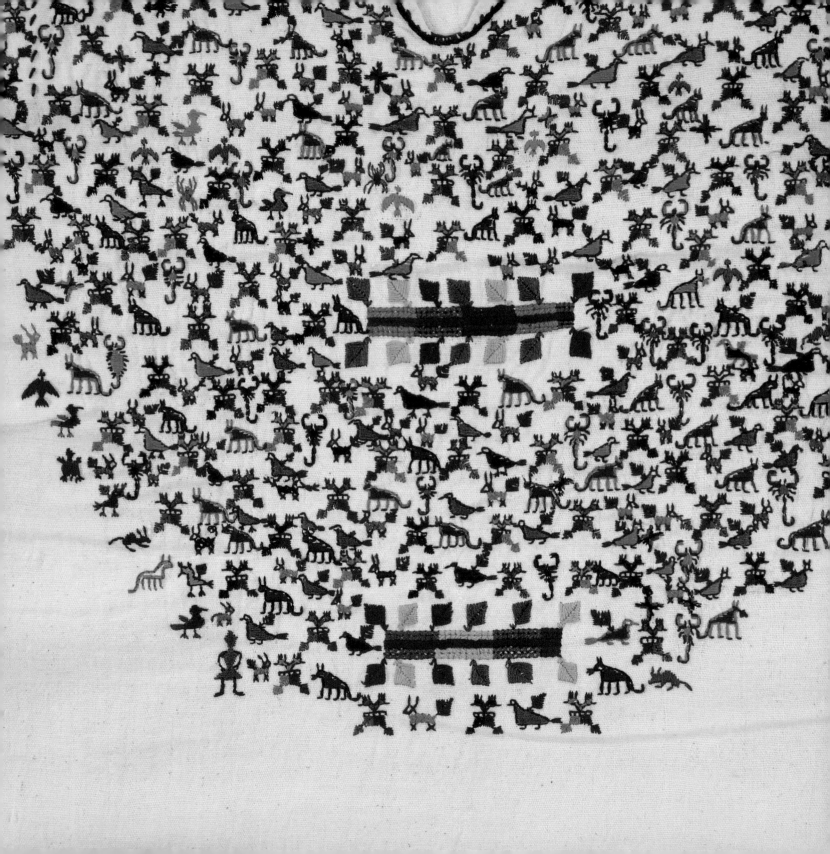

MAN'S SHIRT

Man's shirt, woven from hand-spun cotton on a
backstrap loom, featuring embroidery and drawn threadwork.

The body of the shirt is formed by a single panel of cloth: folded and cut to
make an opening for the head, it is unsewn at the sides. Each rectangular
sleeve panel is joined only at the wrist (right). The shirt is worn looped
over the sash, with the front fold providing a pouch for possessions.
A band of drawn threadwork runs along the shoulder-line; two
horizontal rectangles, also of drawn threadwork, pattern the
chest area. Stylized and multicoloured motifs are worked
in satin, back, cross, herringbone and chain stitches.
149 × 138 cm (58$\frac{1}{2}$ × 54$\frac{1}{2}$ in) across arms

THE SUCCESS OF THIS BEAUTIFUL DESIGN LIES IN ITS EXPLOITATION
OF SCALE. INNUMERABLE MINUSCULE ANIMAL AND INSECT MOTIFS
ARE GROUPED INTO A ROUNDED FORM AT THE TOP OF THE SHIRT.
THIS DENSE AREA OF EMBROIDERY CONSTRASTS WITH THE PLAIN
SLEEVES AND LOWER SHIRT.

HUIPIL (BACK VIEW)
Huipil woven in three panels on a
backstrap loom from cotton, wool and acrylic yarn.

This ankle-length *huipil* hangs down over the skirt and
hides it from view. For ease of movement, when women
are working, it is worn draped over the shoulders. The
huipiles worn by Trique women carry far more decoration
than they did just a few decades ago. Raised bands of
weft-brocading alternate with open-textured
areas of gauze weaving.
123 × 114 cm (48½ × 45 in)

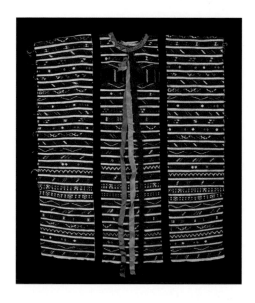

THIS DESIGN BASED ON SIMPLE BANDS IS
ARRESTING BECAUSE OF THE BROAD
ARRAY OF DECORATIVE ELEMENTS. THE
HEAD OPENING IS EMBELLISHED WITH
APPLIQUÉD RIBBON HEMMED IN POINTS
TO EVOKE THE SUN'S RAYS. A COLOURFUL
CASCADE OF RIBBONS HANGS DOWN THE
BACK OF THIS *HUIPIL*.

HUIPIL
This richly embroidered
cotton *huipil* has a square-cut opening for the head.

In recent decades, the *huipiles* of the Mazatec have
increasingly been made from factory cloth. This magnificent
old-style *huipil* was made before 1913, however. Plain- and
gauze-woven on a backstrap loom in two panels, it features
a wide band of brocading along the bottom.
84 × 92 cm (33 × 36 in)

CURVILINEAR BIRDS, RABBITS AND LUSH PLANT DESIGNS HAVE BEEN EMBROIDERED WITH PATTERN DARNING STITCH AND OUTLINE STITCH, CREATING TWO DIFFERENT EFFECTS. THE UPPER USES THE WHITE BASE CLOTH TO DRAW THE OUTLINE OF THE PLANT AND BIRDS, WHEREAS THE LOWER ROW OF BIRDS USES A SIMPLE SILHOUETTE TECHNIQUE. THE BROCADED BORDER, WORKED IN A DIFFERENT STYLE, IS MADE UP OF STYLIZED PLANTS AND GEOMETRIC REPEAT PATTERNING.

HUIPIL
Child's knee-length *huipil* of cotton and artificial silk,
woven in three panels on a backstrap loom, and partially overpainted.

In traditional communities, children's clothing is similar to that worn
by adults. Vivid clusters of weft stripes alternate with rows of raised
geometric motifs brocaded on to a white ground of plain and gauze
weave. The round neckline is reinforced with decorative stitching.
Appliquéd ribbon and braid are used to conceal the panel joins.
87 × 65 cm (34¹/₂ × 25¹/₂ in)

WOMEN IN SAN FELIPE USILA LIKE TO PAINT OVER SELECTED AREAS OF THEIR ORNATE *HUIPILES* WITH AN ANILINE DYE CALLED *FUCHINA*.

INTRICATELY WOVEN DESIGNS ARE GIVEN A COAT OF MUTED PURPLE TO STOP THE SUN FROM 'EATING THE COLOUR OF THE THREADS'.

HUIPIL
Embroidered cotton
huipil, woven in three panels on a backstrap loom.

Bold designs, embroidered in pattern running stitch, dominate areas
of white gauze-woven ground bordered by colourful weft stripes. Cloth
panels are joined with vertical bands of decorative stitching; arm
openings are trimmed to resemble sleeves with crocheted lace and
ribbon. Before the Conquest, Mexican *huipiles* often displayed a small
rectangle in the centre of the chest. Here, a tiny section of
appliquéd ribbon perpetuates this ancient custom.
90 × 92 cm (35$^1/_2$ × 36 in)

DESIGNS ARE ORGANIZED
WITH NEAR PERFECT
SYMMETRY – ONLY THE
COLOUR OF THE CENTRAL
STRIPES BREAKS THE
SYMMETRY. THE STYLIZED
DOUBLE-HEADED BIRDS,

WIDELY THOUGHT TO BE A
PRE-CONQUEST SURVIVAL,
HAVE THE APPEARANCE OF
BROCADED MOTIFS. AS
WITH MANY MEXICAN
TEXTILES, RED IS THE
DOMINANT COLOUR.

HUIPIL
Cotton *huipil*, woven in two panels on a
backstrap loom by the Tzeltal people of Tenejapa, Chiapas

The brocaded motifs were worked with naturally dyed
wool. As in the past, colours are identified with the
cardinal directions. Dyers use a range of fruits,
leaves and other natural dyestuffs, such as
brazilwood. To obtain a rich black, wool
is boiled with a type of iron-rich clay.
158 × 76 cm (62 × 30 in)

IN THE CHIAPAS HIGHLANDS, WHERE DESIGNS PLAY A
SYMBOLIC ROLE, THE *HUIPIL* IS THOUGHT TO ENCLOSE THE
WEAVER IN A SACRED SPACE. FOR THIS BEAUTIFUL *HUIPIL*
THE WEAVER HAS USED THE DOG'S PAW MOTIF, *PATA DE
PERRO*, RENDERED IN A RANGE OF SUBTLE WARM COLOURS.

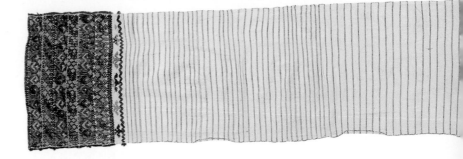

MAN'S SASH (UNDERSIDE AND TOPSIDE)
Tzotzil man's cotton waist-sash, woven on a backstrap
loom. It displays fine weft stripes and brocaded motifs of
wool. Most of the colours were achieved with natural dyes.

Men in Magdalenas wear their richly decorated sashes over
a long shirt. Wrapping them twice round the waist, they
knot them in front with the ends dangling in the
manner of a pre-Conquest loincloth.
209 × 33 cm (82 × 13 in)

THIS SASH INCLUDES THREE ROWS
OF A DESIGN CALLED 'WORMEATEN'
(*CARCOMIDO*). BROCADED ABOVE
BOTH END SECTIONS IS A LINE OF
'SAINTS' (*SANTOS*). THE RANGE OF
WARM COLOURS IS INTERRUPTED
BY THE USE OF BLUE, SEEN MORE
SIGNIFICANTLY ON THE REVERSE
SIDE (BELOW LEFT).

glossary

Acrylics synthetic yarns. One of the best known acrylic fibres is acrilan – a substitute for wool.

Aniline dyes name given to the early synthetic dyes that revolutionized the dyeing industry after 1856.

Appliqué decorative technique whereby supplementary sections of cloth are stitched onto the ground fabric.

Back stitch line of flat stitches, worked from left to right: each stitch touches the previous one.

Backstrap loom portable, body-tensioned loom, also known as a stick loom.

Brazilwood dyewood (*Haematoxylum brasiletto*) that gives purplish-red or deep tan shades.

Brocading weaving technique. Supplementary WEFT (or, more rarely, WARP) threads are used decoratively to create superstructural patterning while cloth is on the loom.

Cards boards inset with short wire bristles, with which wool fibres are rubbed together before being spun.

Chain stitch a series of looped stitches – these form an interlocking line or design filling.

Cochineal red dyestuff obtained from the bodies of insects.

Couching technique whereby threads are laid on the base material and attached by stitching with other threads.

Coyuche, **coyuchi** naturally brown cotton (*Gossypium mexicanum*) from the Náhuatl *coioichcatl*.

Crochet a hooked needle is used to interloop the yarn vertically and horizontally through two loops.

Cross stitch with this type of embroidery, the ground threads are counted. Each cross may be completed individually in two movements. Alternatively rows of single stitches may be done diagonally from left to right, then crossed on the return from right to left.

Drawn threadwork technique whereby individual threads are removed from cloth. The remaining threads are strengthened by binding, often with embroidery threads.

Fishbone stitch two opposing rows of oblique SATIN stitches which slightly overlap in the centre.

Gauze weaving selected WARP threads are crossed and secured by the WEFT, creating an open, lace-like texture.

Herringbone stitch crossed stitch with many variations – simple interlacing stitch.

Hiladillo cochineal-dyed silk.

Huipil woman's sleeveless tunic of pre-Conquest origin (from the Náhuatl *huipilli*).

Ikat this technique takes its name from the Indonesian word *mengikat*, which means to tie. Method used by dyers to pattern yarn before it is woven.

Indigo fast blue dye obtained from various plants of the genus *indigofera*. If indigo is to 'take', exposure to the air is necessary (OXIDIZATION).

Long-armed cross stitch frequently used with cross stitch, stitches resemble a close plait.

Lozenge diamond-shaped design.

Manta calico.

Mercerized cotton shiny treated cotton thread.

Mestizo Mexican of mixed European and Amerindian ancestry.

Mordant substance that combines with and fixes a dyestuff in material that cannot be dyed direct.

Outline stitch *see* STEM STITCH.

Oxidization to combine with oxygen.

Pattern darning stitch counted-thread filling technique worked in RUNNING STITCH.

Plain weaving the simplest possible interlacing of WARP and WEFT in unvarying alternation.

Quechquemitl woman's closed shoulder-cape of pre-Conquest origin (Náhuatl term).

Rebozo woman's rectangular shawl.

Rhomboid LOZENGE-shaped design or parallelogram.

Running stitch flat stitch that involves taking the needle and thread through the cloth at regularly spaced intervals.

Sarape blanket, often with an opening for the head.

Satin stitch flat embroidery stitch. Each stitch is worked parallel to and touching the next.

Servilleta cloth, often used for ceremonial purposes or to cover food.

Shellfish dye purple dye (*Purpura patula pansa*) requiring OXIDIZATION.

Spindle implement for drawing out and twisting fibres into thread. In rural Mexico, yarn is still spun in pre-Conquest fashion: the spinner rapidly rotates the spindle, which has a wooden shaft weighted with a round WHORL.

Stem stitch flat embroidery stitch. The needle is brought out to the left of the stitches that proceed upwards. When the needle is brought out to the right, the stitch is termed OUTLINE.

Stepped fret geometric design, usually repeated to form a decorative band, combining steps with a central scroll or hook. Much used in pre-Conquest Mexico, it may have been a stylization of the serpent.

Tapestry weaving technique for creating designs or pictures in cloth. WEFT threads move across selected areas, not from selvedge to selvedge.

Treadle loom fixed-frame pedal loom, introduced into Mexico from Europe.

Tree of life popular stylized design showing a tree, or pot of flowers, often surrounded by birds. The tree was important in pre-Conquest Mexico, with its roots in the underworld and its branches reaching into the heavens.

Warp threads that stretch lengthways in a fabric.

Warp-faced term describing cloth where the WARP threads lie so closely together that they cover the WEFT.

Warp patterning WARP threads periodically cross varying numbers of WEFT threads to create raised designs in the cloth.

Weft transverse threads that interlace with the WARP.

Weft-faced term used to describe cloth where the WEFT completely covers the WARP. This happens with TAPESTRY.

Whorl disk of clay or wood on the lower part of the SPINDLE.

selected reading

Albers, A., *On Weaving*, Studio Vista, 1974

Anawalt, P.R., *Indian Clothing before Cortés: Mesoamerican Costumes from the Codices,* University of Oklahoma Press, 1981

Anaya, Y. *et al, La magia de los hilos: Arte y tradición en el textil de Veracruz,* Universidad Veracruzana, 1995

Balfour-Paul, J., *Indigo,* British Museum Press, 1998

Benson Gyles, A. and C. Sayer, *Of Gods and Men: Mexico and the Mexican Indian,* BBC Publications, 1980

Bernstein, S. (ed.), *Mirrors of the Gods: Proceedings of a Symposium on the Huichol Indians,* San Diego Museum Papers No. 25, 1989

Blum Schevill, M., *Costume as Communication,* Haffenreffer Museum of Anthropology, Brown University, 1986

Burnham, D.K., *Warp and Weft: A Textile Terminology,* Royal Ontario Museum, 1980

Calderon de la Barca, F., *Life in Mexico... (1843),* Dent and Sons, 1970

Castelló Yturbide, T., *Colorantes naturales de México,* Industrias Resistol, 1988

Castelló Yturbide, T. *et al, El rebozo,* Artes de México (Número 142), 1971

Clabburn, P., *The Needleworker's Dictionary,* William Morrow & Co., Inc., 1976

Cordry, D.B. and D.M., *Mexican Indian Costumes,* University of Texas Press, 1968

Covarrubias, M., *Mexico South: The Isthmus of Tehuantepec,* Alfred A. Knopf, 1946

Donkin, R.A., 'Spanish Red: An Ethnographical Study of Cochineal and the Opuntia Cactus', Transactions of the American Philosophical Society 67 (5), 1977

Duby, G., *Chiapas indígena,* Universidad Nacional Autónoma de México, 1961

Enciso, J., *Design Motifs of Ancient Mexico,* Dover Publications Inc., 1953
Designs from Pre-Columbian Mexico, Dover Publications Inc., 1971

Field, F., *Pre-Hispanic Mexican Stamp Designs,* Dover Publications Inc., 1974

Fischgrund Stanton, A., *Zapotec Weavers of Teotitlán,* Museum of New Mexico Press, 1999

Fomento Cultural Banamex, A.C., *Grandes maestros del arte popular mexicano,* 1998

Fundación Cultural Serfin, *Colorantes milenarios en el textil indígena,* 1997

Harris, J. (ed.), *5000 Years of Textiles,* British Museum Press, 1993

Hecht, A., *The Art of the Loom: Weaving, Spinning and Dyeing across the World,* British Museum Press, 1989

Jeter, J. and P.M. Juelke, *The Saltillo Sarape* (exhibition catalogue), Santa Barbara Museum of Art, 1978

Johnson, I.W., 'Vestido y adorno', *Lo efímero y lo eterno del arte popular mexicano* I: 161–267, Fondo Editorial de la Plástica Mexicana, 1971
'Basketry and Textiles': *Handbook of Middle American Indians* 10, University of Texas Press, 1971
Design Motifs on Mexican Indian Textiles (2 vols.), Akademische Druck und Verlagsanstalt, 1976

Johnson, I.W., *et al, El textil mexicano: Linea y color,* Museo Rufino Tamayo, 1986

Lechuga, R.D., *El traje indígena de México,* Panorama

Editorial S.A., 1982

Textil tradicional de Veracruz, Instituto de Artes
Plásticas, Universidad Veracruzana, 1994

Lechuga, R.D. *et al, Textiles de Oaxaca,* Artes de México
(Número 35), 1996

Logan, I. *et al, Rebozos de la Colección Robert Everts,*
Museo Franz Mayer y Artes de México, 1995

Lumholtz, C., *Unknown Mexico* (2 vols), Macmillan and Co.,
1903

McEwan, C., *Ancient Mexico in the British Museum,* British
Museum Press, 1994

Mapelli Mozzi, C. and T. Castelló Yturbide, *El traje indígena
en México* (2 vols), INAH-SEP, 1965–8

La tejedora de vida, Banca Serfin, 1987

Morris, W.F., *A Millennium of Weaving in Chiapas,* Sna
Jolobil, 1984

Living Maya, Harry N. Abrahams Inc., 1987

Orellana, M. de *et al, Textiles de Chiapas,* Artes de México
(Número 19), 1993

Paine, S., *Embroidered Textiles: Traditional Patterns from
Five Continents,* Thames & Hudson, 1990

Past, A., Bon: *Tintes naturales,* Sna Jolobil, 1980

Sahagún, Fray B. de, *Codex Florentino: General History of
the Things of New Spain,* ed., trans. A.J.O. Anderson and
C.E. Dibble. Monographs (14) parts 2–13. University of
Utah and School of American Research, 1950–69

Sayer, C., *Crafts of Mexico,* Aldus Books, 1977

Mexican Textile Techniques, Shire Books, 1988

Arts and Crafts of Mexico, Thames & Hudson,
1990

Mexican Patterns: A Design Source Book, Studio
Editions, 1990

Mexican Textiles, British Museum Press, 1998
(Published in 1985 in the UK as *Mexican
Costume* and in the USA as *Costumes of Mexico*)

Scheffler, L., *Grupos indígenas de México,* Panorama
Editorial S.A., 1989

Schele. L. and M.E. Miller, *The Blood of Kings: Dynasty and
Ritual in Maya Art,* George Braziller and Kimbell Art
Museum, 1986

Seiler-Baldinger, A., *Textiles: A Classification of
Techniques,* Crawford House Press, 1994

Start, L.E., *The McDougall Collection of Indian Textiles
from Guatemala and Mexico,* Occasional Papers on
Technology 2, Pitt Rivers Museum, University of Oxford,
1980

Turok, M., 'Diseño y simbolo en el huipil ceremonial de
Magdalenas, Chiapas', *Boletín 3,* Sep, 1974

Turok, M. *et al, El caracol púrpura: una tradición milenaria
de Oaxaca,* Dirección General de Culturas Populares,
1988

Tylor, Sir E.B., *Anahuac: or Mexico and the Mexicans,
Ancient and Modern,* Longman Green, Longman and
Roberts, 1861

Wade, N.V., *The Basic Stitches of Embroidery,* Victoria &
Albert Museum, 1966

museum accession numbers

PAGE   ACC. NO.

2	1985 Am 34.4
4	1997 Am 4.1
7	1978 Am 15.4b (top)
7	1977 Am 34.1 (left)
7	1987 Am 7.135 (right)
7	1978 Am 15.12 (below)
22	1996 Am 10.2
24	1996 Am 15.26
25	1978 Am 15.302b
26	1977 Am 34.1
30	1986 Am 7.124
32	1986 Am 7.111
34	1978 Am 15.152
36	1978 Am 15.153
38	1987 Am 7.166
40	1986 Am 7.135
42	1978 Am 15.4b
46	1997 Am 4.1
48	1986 Am 6.16
50	1982 Am 3.8b
52	1978 Am 15.174h
53	1978 Am 15.175c (top)
53	1978 Am 15.175d (below)
54	1996 Am 10.7
56	1996 Am 10.9
58	1996 Am 10.5
60	1995 Am 12.1
62	1978 Am 15.50
64	1977 Am 7.1
66	1977 Am 7.2
68	1977 Am 7.4a
70	1978 Am 15.1a
72	Q72 Am 15
74	1981 Am 22.1
78	1985 Am 34.3
80	1985 Am 34.7

The textiles on pp.22, 46, 54, 56, 58 are from the Robert Evert's collection.

publisher's acknowledgements

The textiles featured in this book are drawn from the collections of the British Museum's Department of Ethnography and have been selected from the viewpoint of their design and technical merit.

We should like to express our thanks to the many people who have helped us in the production of this book, and in particular from the Museum staff: Helen Wolfe, Abigail Hampton, Imogen Laing and David Agar. Paul Welti, the art director, must be credited not only for his arresting juxtaposition of illustrations and text, but also for his contribution to the captions analyzing the designs.

author's acknowedgements

I would like to thank Ruth D. Lechuga and Irmgard Weitlaner Johnson for generously sharing their knowledge with me over many years. This book celebrates the artistry of Mexico's many weavers, dyers and embroiderers. Ana Cecilia Cruz Alberto and Francisca Rivera Pérez are among the many who have explained and demonstrated their techniques with infinite patience. I would also like to thank Ofelia López Méndez and Las Mujeres Unidas para el Desarrollo de Chiapas. I am grateful to Jesús Candelario Cosío and the Huichol community of Tierras Blancas.

index

Acatlán 6, 18, 43–5
acrylics 13, 16, 17, 24, 71, 82
Aguascalientes 60
aniline dyes 60, 74, 82
appliqué 74, 76, 82
artificial silk 18, 38, 48, 74
Aztecs 9, 20

back stitch 69, 82
bedspreads 6, 12, 16, 26–9
blankets see sarape
blouses 10, 13, 18, 31, 38
braid 74
brazilwood 57, 79, 82
brocading 6, 10, 15, 16, 24, 26, 40, 60, 64, 66, 71, 73, 74, 79, 80, 82

calico (manta) 53, 83
chain stitch 69, 82
Chiapas 8, 10, 11, 12, 13, 15, 19–20, 79
Chinantec 8, 18, 74–7
cloths 6, 23, 35, 37
    servilleta 12, 83
Coahuila 16–17, 54–8
cochineal 14, 57, 64, 66, 82
cotton 11, 12, 13, 14, 24–31, 38, 52, 64, 69, 71, 73, 74, 76, 79
couching 43, 82
coyuche (coyuchi) 12–13, 82
crochet 76, 82
cross stitch 18, 23, 40, 51, 52, 53, 69, 82
Cruz Alberto, Ana Cecilia 16, 26
Cuetzalan 12, 13

drawn threadwork 18, 69, 82
dyeing 13–14, 46, 60
dyes 13–14, 43, 57, 60, 64, 66, 74, 79, 82

eagle 18, 43, 50, 52, 62

embroidery 10, 11, 13, 17–18, 21, 31, 34–45, 50–3, 69, 73, 76

fishbone stitch 18, 82
flowers
fringes 18, 24–5, 46, 48, 58, 60
fuchina 74

gala costume 17
gauze weaving 13, 16, 71, 73, 82
Guerrero 6, 9, 18, 42–5

herringbone stitch 23, 51, 69, 82
Hidalgo 6, 9, 33–5
hiladillo 14, 64, 66, 82
Huichol 6, 8, 9, 11, 18, 19, 20, 51, 53
huipil 9, 10, 13, 15, 17, 18, 62–4, 71–9, 74, 82

ikat 46, 48, 82
indigo 14, 43, 57, 66, 82

Jalisco 6, 9, 51, 53

lace 17, 76
long-armed cross stitch 23, 51, 52, 53, 82
looms 15, 16, 82, 83
lozenges 54, 60, 83

Magdalenas 20, 80
marriage clothes 64
Maya 8, 20 see also Tzeltal, Tzotzil
Mazahua 22–4
Mazatec 8, 73
Mendoza, Arnulfo 17
mercerized cotton 17, 35, 37, 83
Mestizo 46–8, 54–60, 83
Michoacán 25
Mixtec 8, 13, 14, 15, 62–6
mordants 13, 83

Nahua 6, 9, 10, 12, 13, 18, 40–5

Oaxaca 8, 11, 13, 14, 17, 18, 64–77
ombré dyeing 60
Otomí 6, 10, 11, 16, 18, 20, 26–37
overpainting 18, 74

pattern boards 57
pattern darning stitch 83
patterns and motifs 16–17, 18–20, 23, 43, 51, 53, 60, 76, 79, 81
peyote 20, 52, 53
Pinotepa de Don Luis 14, 66
pom-poms 18
Puebla 9, 10, 12, 13, 16, 18, 31–2
Purépecha 25

quechquemitl 6, 9, 10, 13, 16, 17, 18, 19, 32, 40, 51, 83

rayon 13
rebozo 10, 11, 14, 18, 46–8, 83
ribbons 18, 74, 76
Rivera Pérez, Francisca 13
running stitch 18, 31, 38, 76, 83

sacatinta 14
Saltillo 16–17, 54–8
San Andrés Chicahuaxtla 71
San Andrés Cohamiata 53
San Andrés Tzicuilan 13
San Bartolomé Ayautla 73
San Felipe Usila 18, 74
San Juan Chamula 14
San Luis Potosí 9, 10, 46–8
San Miguel Ameyalco 6, 16, 26
San Miguel Metlatonoc 62
San Pablito 11, 18, 20, 31–2
San Pedro Jicayán 64

Santa María del Río 10, 14, 18, 46–8
Santa María Zacatepec 19, 69
sarape 11, 16–17, 54–61, 83
satin stitch 6, 17–18, 35, 37, 43, 69, 83
shawls see rebozo
shellfish dye 14, 64, 66, 83
shirts 11, 53, 69
shoulder-bags 11, 18, 52
silk 11, 13, 17
skirts 9
    wrap-around 6, 10, 17, 18, 43–5, 66
Spanish Conquest 9, 11, 17
spindles 12, 13, 83
spinning 12, 13–14
stem stitch 18, 83
stepped frets 18, 32, 83

tablecloth 12, 23
Tacuate 69
tapestry weaving 16–17, 54–61, 83
tassels 18
Tenango de Doria 6, 18, 35–7
Tenejapa 10, 79
tree of life 83
Trique 8, 71
trousers 11, 53
Tzeltal 10, 79
Tzotzil 4, 10, 12, 14, 15, 80

Veracruz 9, 40

waist-sashes 9, 11, 13, 18, 24–5, 80–1
warp 15, 83
weaving 13, 15–17, 32, 54–61, 71, 73, 82, 83
weft 15, 60, 83
wool 12–14, 16, 25, 32, 57, 58, 71, 80

Zapatistas 20
Zapotec 8, 17

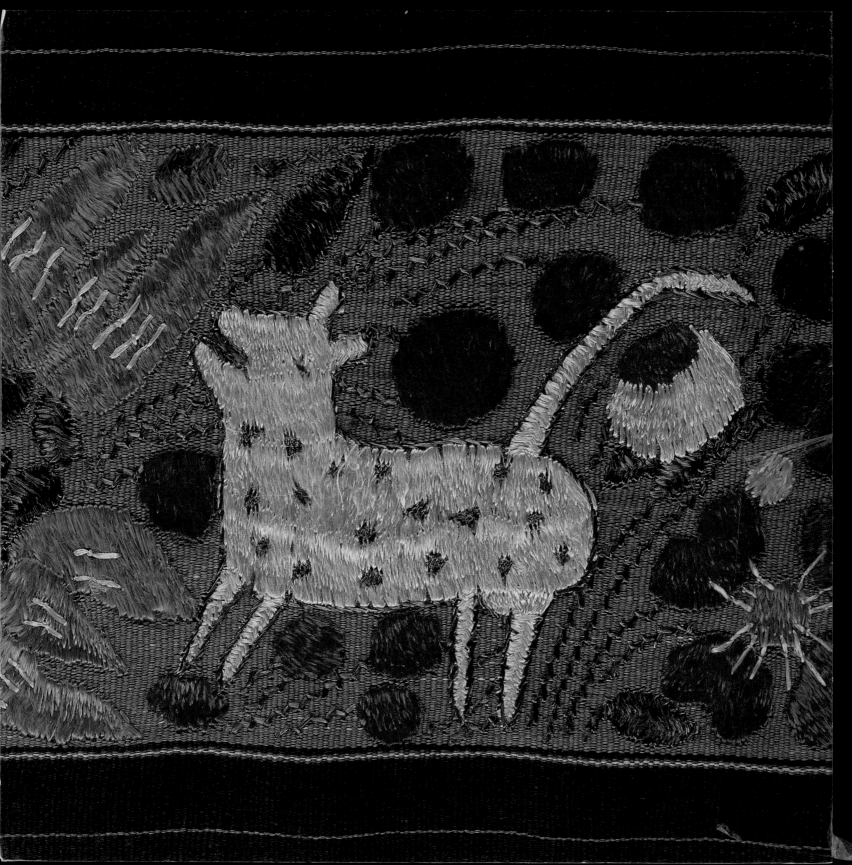